Dream Crazy Big!

THE JOJO SIWA STORY

Katy Sprinkel

30 YEARS
TRIUMPH
BOOKS

This book is available in quantity at special discounts for your group or organization. For further information, contact:

Triumph Books LLC
814 North Franklin Street
Chicago, Illinois 60610
(312) 337-0747
www.triumphbooks.com

Printed in U.S.A.
ISBN: 978-1-62937-800-8

Content written, developed, and packaged by Katy Sprinkel
Edited by Laine Morreau
Design and page production by Patricia Frey
Cover design by Preston Pisellini

Title page photograph and illustrations courtesy of iStock; remaining photographs courtesy of Getty Images.

Contents

Chapter One
Girls Just Want to Have Fun
9

Chapter Two
All She Wants to Do Is Dance
25

Chapter Three
Voices Carry
41

Chapter Four
Electric Avenue
57

Chapter Five
Express Yourself
73

Chapter Six
She Works Hard for the Money
87

Chapter Seven
Sweet Dreams (Are Made of This)
103

Girls Just Want to Have Fun

For as long as she can remember, JoJo Siwa wanted to be a pop star.

And at the age of 16, JoJo has already achieved a level of fame most performers will never come close to reaching. She first became a household name at age nine, when she was a featured dancer on *Abby's Ultimate Dance Competition*, performing for the notoriously demanding Abby Lee Miller. She continued on with Miller on *Dance Moms* before following her own star onward.

As a YouTuber, JoJo gained a generation of new fans who eagerly awaited her lighthearted and high-energy posts. Her unpredictability and excitability catapulted her into megastardom on the site (she has more than 10 million subscribers as of this writing). That in turn caught the attention of Nickelodeon, who signed the star to a deal with the network.

But JoJo's on-screen achievements are only part of the picture. She's an emerging recording artist—"Boomerang" is RIAA certified platinum, and its music video has more than 743 million YouTube views at last count. And she's a master merchandiser too. You'll find JoJo's products everywhere from department stores to grocery stores to e-tailers.

Smiling like a kid in a candy store during a 2019 tour stop.

With her dog BowBow in 2018.

JoJo is also a passionate voice against bullying. Her iconic hair bows telegraph that principle: anyone who wears a JoJo bow will not tolerate bullying, period. It's a powerful message that has made the bows, and JoJo, a giant success story.

The sky is the limit for JoJo, who seems to have the Midas touch whenever she turns her attention to a new project. And Siwanatorz—the self-dubbed name of her legion of fans—can't wait to see what comes next.

To trace JoJo's incredible rise to fame, it's important to begin at the beginning. It was May 19, 2003, when parents Tom and Jessalynn and older brother Jayden welcomed a little girl, Joelle Joanie Siwa, into the world. A far cry from Hollywood, the Siwa family lived in Omaha, Nebraska. Tom was a practicing chiropractor and Jessalynn owned her own dance school.

Did You Know?

Dance *really* runs in the family. Jessalynn's parents were ballroom dance instructors.

Dream Crazy Big!
The JoJo Siwa Story

In a sense, JoJo was born into show business naturally. She spent long hours in her mom's dance studio watching the other kids perfect their routines. She saw firsthand how much work went into achieving excellence as a dancer, the time and commitment required. She understood innately that not everyone has what it takes to be a success, that it's one thing to have a dream and another to chase after it with all you have.

She also got a head start most dancers could only dream of: full-time access to a dance instructor (that's you, Mom) and studio space. "When my husband would come pick her up at the [dance] studio, she would not want to leave at night," Jessalynn told *Rolling Stone* in a 2019 interview. At home, JoJo would pirouette around the kitchen while her mom cooked her mac and cheese. Her reputation as a dancer preceded her even then; her proud parents would drag her out of bed occasionally to perform dances at houseguests' behest.

Little wonder, then, that she was onstage in front of audiences from a very early age. At one and a half, JoJo was included in Jessalynn's student showcases. She'd perform what her mom calls "the hottie dance" while Jessalynn rained down glitter on her. JoJo performed her first solo dance at age two, still in diapers, at the prestigious Kids Artistic Revue. It was a precocious routine set to *Hairspray*'s "Mama, I'm a Big Girl Now."

JoJo often calls her mom her best friend.

Grabbing a quick selfie on the red carpet in 2016.

It's easy to see the spark of joy in JoJo in even that early performance. Don't believe it? That first solo dance lives on 24/7 on JoJo's YouTube channel, ItsJoJoSiwa. (Check out https://www.youtube.com/watch?v=hrjHrbV8u3k for the mega-cuteness!)

JoJo often says that as early as she can remember, she wanted to be a star. "I was three years old and I saw *Hannah Montana*. I was like, 'I want to be Hannah Montana,'" she confessed on *The Tonight Show Starring Jimmy Fallon* in 2019. "And everyone wants to be Hannah Montana," she continued, "but I was like, 'Really, I want to do this.'" And she set out to do just that.

But that didn't mean JoJo spent *all* her time practicing. She still found time to be a normal kid. Summers in Nebraska were spent grilling out, swimming in the backyard with her brother, and competing with her family in games and water-gun fights. She loved movies, her dogs, and crafting.

Fun Fact
Long before they were known as JoJo bows, JoJo and her mom made her distinctive hair bows themselves.

Dream Crazy Big!
The JoJo Siwa Story

"My parents were all about family values and making sure we stay grounded," JoJo wrote in her autobiography, *JoJo's Guide to the Sweet Life*. That meant lots of family time, and those early days in Omaha were filled with music, laughter, and fun. They loved to tease each other and play practical jokes (still do, as JoJo's YouTube followers know all too well).

With a strong support system, incredible work ethic, and the fire to succeed, a young JoJo was poised for big things. Little did she know that opportunity would knock so early... ★

It's a family affair for the Siwas, in attendance at JoJo's 16th birthday party.

"I feel like every day is my wedding day," says Jessalynn about JoJo's overwhelming success.

The Stars Shine Bright in Omaha

JoJo's not the only boldfaced name to hail from Nebraska's biggest city. Omaha is the hometown of everyone from Hollywood royalty such as Marlon Brando and the Fonda family to political titans such as former US president Gerald Ford and Malcolm X. "The Oracle of Omaha," billionaire Warren Buffett, calls Omaha home. Musicians including Bright Eyes' Conor Oberst, singer-songwriter Elliott Smith, and the band 311 all hail from Omaha. It's spawned funny people too—such as actor and comedian Adam Devine and filmmaker Alexander Payne, just to name a couple. And is it any coincidence that one of the most famous dancers of all time, Fred Astaire, was an Omahan?

JoJo shares dancing grace with Astaire...

...goofiness with Devine...

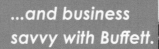

...and business savvy with Buffett.

"My family is awesome. They keep me grounded—they keep me normal.... To them I'm not some celebrity kid, I'm not some famous kid. To them, I'm just my brother's little sister, I'm my dad's little girl, I'm my mom's little kid." —JoJo to Fox News

chapter two

All She Wants to Do Is Dance

JoJo got her first big break in show business without even knowing it.

She was working hard toward her dream as a dancer, and flourishing in local competitions and showcases, when Jessalynn caught notice of a casting call for a reality show dance competition. Without mentioning it to JoJo, she sent in a tape of her daughter's performances. Producers liked what they saw in the plucky seven-year-old and requested an audition via Skype.

The show was *Abby's Ultimate Dance Competition*, and both JoJo and Jessalynn were ultimately cast to join the program. A sort of dance version of then-hot singing show *American Idol*, it featured the notoriously demanding Abby Lee Miller of *Dance Moms* fame. And with that, JoJo was immediately thrust into the spotlight, beamed into the living rooms of millions of TV viewers across the country.

AUDC was, to put it bluntly, intense. The contestants had to learn a new dance every three days, which meant cramming a lot of rehearsals into a tiny amount of time. Not one to take it easy on her dancers, Miller threw JoJo a huge curveball for her

JoJo shows off some of her moves for students of the Abby Lee Dance Company during a 2019 appearance at Miller's studio.

Portrait of the artist as a young dancer; JoJo in 2016.

first dance. Set to *Rapunzel*, she would have to dance in a long, heavy wig that was sewn into her hair. Suffice it to say, it was nothing the seven-year-old had encountered to that point. Happily, that first dance was a triumph, and JoJo was off and running.

By the Numbers

According to JoJo, **hundreds** of hours of footage were filmed to produce one hourlong episode of *Dance Moms*.

She became incredibly close with her fellow contestants on *AUDC*, who spent day and night together. It was "like being at summer camp with all your favorite people," she wrote in her autobiography. Unfortunately, that made contestant eliminations extremely painful. "Every three days we cried," she continued.

The competition was difficult, unpredictable, and cutthroat. The dances ran the gamut of styles, from classical to modern, playing to dancers' strengths and weaknesses in equal measure. In order to succeed, the dancers needed to be disciplined, dedicated, and pitch-perfect. Any mistakes, and it could be their last dance. JoJo outlasted most of the competition, falling in the week before the final elimination. But the lessons she learned on the show cemented her strong work ethic, dedication, and the thick skin she'd need in show business.

She may have lost on *Abby's Ultimate Dance Competition*, but her talent, determination, and sparkling personality won her an even bigger prize: a spot on the show *Dance Moms* and the opportunity to join the Abby Lee Dance Company. She and her mom were cast on the series' fourth season. When they got the call, they were told they needed to be there in two days. It was a big decision, because it meant breaking up the family. Jessalynn and JoJo moved to Los Angeles, and Tom and Jayden stayed back in Omaha. While it was hard on the Siwa family, it was the realization of JoJo's ultimate goal—as a dancer, a *Dance Moms* superfan (since day one!), and a girl dead-set on becoming a superstar.

"*Dance Moms* [changed] everything," JoJo wrote in her autobiography. Often grueling, usually emotional, JoJo's seasons as a reality star always made for must-see TV. They were also critical learning years in which JoJo built a solid foundation for success.

Fans of the show can chart her every up and down on the pyramid during her three-season span (and new Siwanatorz who missed it the first time around can stream every episode

Posing with Dance Moms costars (from left) Kendall Vertes, Brynn Ashlee Rumfallo, and Kalani Hilliker at the 2016 Teen Choice Awards.

Glammed up at the 2016 Women of Excellence event.

> "[Performing] is definitely in her blood. I knew the moment that I was having a girl that she was going to be a dancer and that she was going to wear bows and tutus and she was going to like it."
>
> —Jessalynn to *Today*

on Lifetime). Whether you loved her or hated her, the chatterbox with the big bows in her hair always captured viewers' attention. And her tenure on the show opened up some huge doors for her in Hollywood. (More on that later.)

Giving credit where credit is due, she frequently cites Miller as a huge influence on her career. When asked by *People* in 2017 about the lessons she learned from Miller, she said, "She teaches you how to sink or swim…. I have a lot to thank her for."

Despite their tumultuous on-screen relationship—they had lots of friction on the show!—JoJo has stood by Miller through the embattled reality maven's toughest times, including recent

33

Dream Crazy Big!
The JoJo Siwa Story

legal and health struggles. And when Miller made a rare public appearance to attend JoJo's sweet 16 birthday party, she had nothing but sweetness and light for her former student. When asked by E! if she could believe JoJo's incredible success, she replied emphatically, "Of course, come on! A great work ethic, always pleasant, always fun to work with… she's doing great."

Count Miller as one of the original Siwanatorz. Without her help, JoJo might never have become, well, JoJo! ★

JoJo and her dancers are in sync during a 2019 tour stop.

Top 10 JoJo-related quotes
from *AUDC* and *Dance Moms*

10. "Less talking and more dancing." —Abby Lee Miller to JoJo

9. "I would love to do this [Michael Jackson] solo because I *am* MJ." —JoJo

8. "You're JoJo, you can handle it, just do what you do." —JoJo

7. "I'm amazing, and I'm going to top everyone else." —JoJo

6. "We came here to be permanent members of the ALDC, and we're not leaving until that happens." —Jessalynn

5. "I invited JoJo [back] to Pittsburgh because I want [the dancers] to see what it takes to be a star." —Miller, upon JoJo's *DM* visit in Season 8

4. "What you have, JoJo, is wonderful, and [the other dancers] don't have any of it." —Miller

3. "I'm loud and I have a voice and I'm going to use it." —JoJo

2. "I would say it's my mission in life to make JoJo a star." —Jessalynn

1. "You guys don't understand. [Abby] said...I...I can't wear bows to dance!" —JoJo

Though they often clashed on TV, JoJo calls Abby Lee Miller a mentor and a friend.

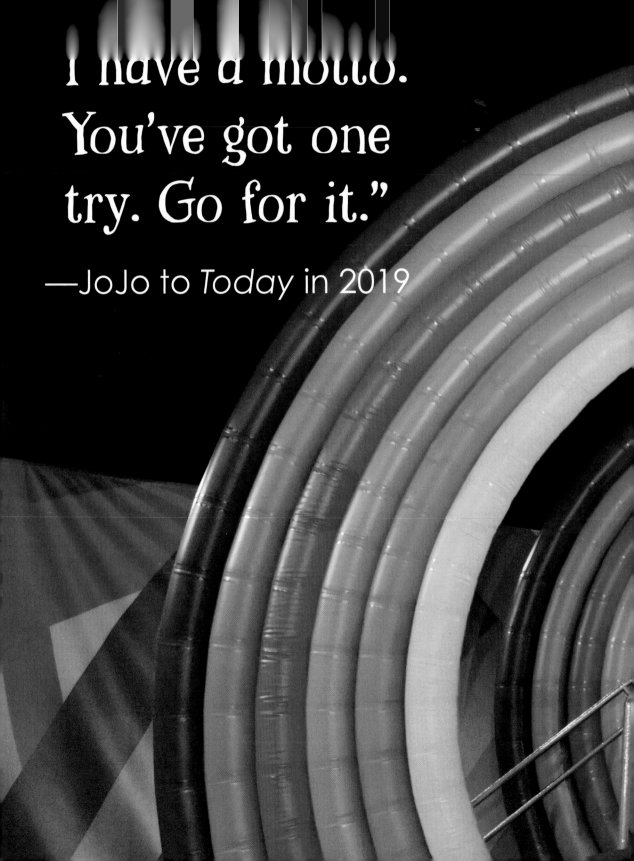

I have a motto. You've got one try. Go for it."

—JoJo to *Today* in 2019

chapter three

Voices Carry

Directly or indirectly, it was Abby Lee Miller who first showed JoJo the power that social media can have.

Unfortunately, it was a negative experience that first got JoJo's attention. After an airing of *Abby's Ultimate Dance Competition*, Miller reached out to her Instagram followers, asking who should be eliminated in the next episode. A number of people said JoJo, many of them harshly. It was the first time JoJo came face-to-face with the ugliest of Internet dwellers: the troll.

Facing criticism can be hard for anybody, but facing nameless, faceless criticism is brutal. Especially for someone as young as JoJo was. The nine-year-old came to her mother in tears, and Jessalynn gave her advice that would change JoJo's life forever: Why devote time and energy to the people who have negative things to say about you when there are so many people saying positive things? Listening to the haters gives them power; tuning them out and listening to your friends, family, and people who support you empowers you.

JoJo first joined social media while a regular on *Dance Moms*. With it, she gave viewers a glimpse into her world as a

JoJo takes over the Young Hollywood Tour on November 16, 2018.

Celebrating her 15th birthday with pal Colleen Ballinger (aka Miranda Sings).

touring competitive dancer and, more important, showed the goofy side of her that wasn't readily apparent on the drama-centric TV show. She performed silly stunts and dances. She showered herself with countless juices (the primary conceit of her *JoJo's Juice* series, each installment concluding with a Nickelodeon sliming–style

By the Numbers

There's a reason why JoJo is an undisputed social media titan! As of this writing, she has **8.8 million** Instagram followers and **10.3 million** YouTube subscribers.

barrage of a different beverage). She interacted with other YouTubers, including Miranda Sings (becoming besties with her real-life alter ego, Colleen Ballinger). There are countless practical jokes and pranks, up-to-the-minute updates on every aspect of JoJo's world, and lots of BowBow cuteness. It was— and remains—a candy-colored, gleeful celebration of the best things about being a kid.

She also took the time to interact directly with her subscribers, answering their questions in a regular Q&A feature. The questions were often light, but it wasn't all fun and games. She wasn't afraid to talk to her fans about difficult topics too. Reflecting on the lesson she learned from that first hurtful

Dream Crazy Big!
The JoJo Siwa Story

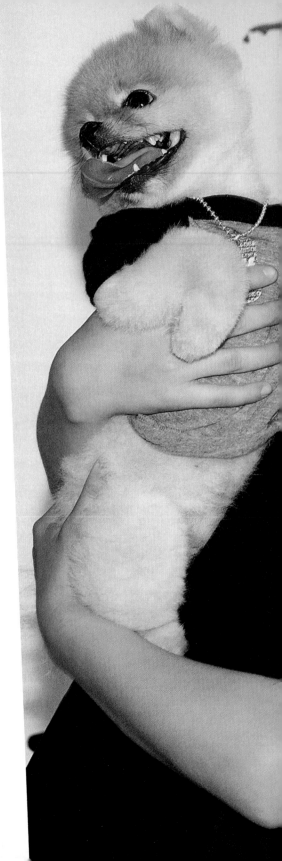

online experience, she often took the time to get serious about haters.

JoJo's candor and transparency endeared her to fans and parents alike, and her YouTube views kept climbing higher and higher. She got a manager—Caryn Sterling, who is still with her today—who helped her take another step forward in her career. She signed a merchandising deal with accessories giant Claire's, who would produce and sell her bows nationwide. Ultimately her hair bows—that signature accent that had been a constant in her on- and off-screen life—came to symbolize tolerance itself.

Writing on social media in 2017, JoJo explained how her bows could be an agent for change. "What does wearing a JoJo bow mean to

46

Showing her goofy side on the red carpet in 2015.

"It's a very hard goal, but what I want is to tell people who are getting bullied to stand up to the bully and not let it be OK—tell a teacher, the principal or your parents. I want people to stand up and to be confident."
—JoJo to J-14

> "I never forget where I came from with YouTube. I wouldn't be where I am today without it."
>
> —JoJo to *Rolling Stone*

you?" she asked her followers. "To me it means 1. [You're] confident, you believe in yourself and others 2. You say no to bullying and other people can look at us and know that we're kind and will be their friend 3. You like to have fun, stand out and are NEVER afraid to be different."

It was the kernel of an idea that blossomed into a movement. By now, JoJo has made a career out of promoting the fight against bullying. Her first single, "Boomerang"—which she cowrote when she was just twelve years old—supports that vision. It's a call to action for kids everywhere. Everyone gets bullied sometimes, she realized. There's no way to stop it, but there is a way to render bullies powerless: don't listen to them! It's the crux of the song and JoJo's platform. *I don't really care about what they say / Imma come back like a boomerang*, she intones.

"'Boomerang' means a lot to me—it isn't just a song. It's a way for me—and every girl—to be strong against bullies," JoJo wrote in her autobiography. The music video is classic

Dream Crazy Big!
The JoJo Siwa Story

JoJo—all rainbows and sparkles and lots and lots of bows. And the extra-special touch is that she recruited all of her real-life friends to appear in the video alongside her—both her hometown friends and *Dance Moms* pals. "It was so amazing to be surrounded by my best friends in the world while singing about how to stand up [to] bullies *together*," she continued.

The song was a smash—earning platinum status from the Recording Industry Association of America. As of this writing, it has 768 million views on JoJo's YouTube channel alone. And it remains the anthem for Siwanatorz everywhere.

JoJo's social media remains a safe haven for her multitude of fans (she regularly eclipses 2 million views a day). It's a loving, supportive realm where negativity is the exception, not the rule. Through her media and her message, JoJo has built an online community of Siwanatorz where, true to the lyrics of "Boomerang," they don't let the haters get their way. ★

> "Everyone wants to be their best self, and JoJo makes them feel like it's okay to be that way."
>
> —Jessalynn to *Today*

Things are looking up for the young star.

Kindness Rules!

Siwanatorz: heed JoJo's example. A little kindness can go a long way. Not sure where to start? Here are a couple ideas to get you going.

First things first: happiness is contagious! Something as simple as a smile can go a long way. Whether it's welcoming someone to sit with you at lunch or play at recess, a smile signals to others that you are kind and approachable.

Are you crafty? Paint some rocks (smooth, flat ones work best) with kind and inspirational messages (such as "Be Yourself" or "You Rock!"). Then you can scatter them around your neighborhood. They're sure to put a smile on the face of the person who happens upon them!

Have you outgrown some of your clothes or toys? There are always people in need! Instead of letting that stuff pile up, why not donate it to a kid who could use it? There are probably tons of local charities that accept donations in your area. Ask your parents or teacher for help finding the right place.

Do you have a special skill? Maybe you're great at playing double Dutch or drawing pictures. If you see someone struggling who could use your help, why not offer it?

Notice something that you admire or like? Instead of just thinking it, say it! Maybe you like someone's shoes or you're impressed by how fast she can run. Whatever it might be, paying a compliment to someone always makes her day.

And remember, grown-ups need kindness too! Take the time to tell someone you know that you appreciate them!

"Just be kind. The act itself, it's free. And it's priceless."
—Lady Gaga

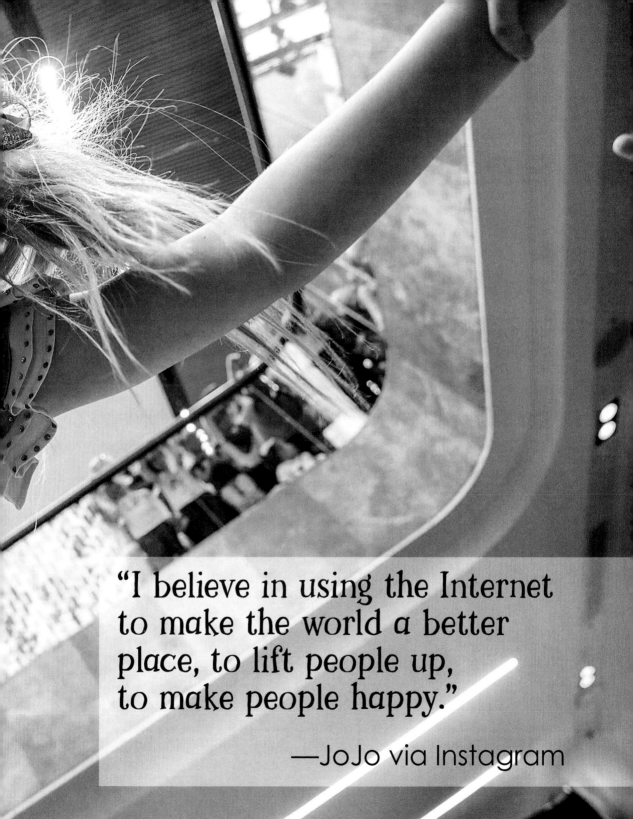

"I believe in using the Internet to make the world a better place, to lift people up, to make people happy."

—JoJo via Instagram

chapter four

Electric Avenue

JoJo and Jessalynn left the drama of *Dance Moms* in the show's sixth season.

Owing to the viral success of "Boomerang" and JoJo's firmly cemented status as a YouTube influencer, Nickelodeon approached JoJo and signed her to a multiplatform deal with the network that included not just TV but merchandising, music, social media, and touring.

She's a frequent fixture on the network. She cohosts *Lip Sync Battle Shorties* with Nick Cannon. She's given viewers a backstage pass to her crazy life through specials about everything from her sweet 16 birthday party to her world tour. She's even done a bit of acting, appearing in shows and movies including *The Thundermans*, *School of Rock*, *Middle School Moguls*, and *Nickelodeon's Sizzling Summer Camp Special*. But that's not all. JoJo and her dog, BowBow, also have animated avatars. *The JoJo and BowBow Show Show* follows the cartoon adventures—and misadventures—of JoJo and her "best friend," her beloved teacup Yorkie.

Resurrecting a Double Dare stunt at 2018 VidCon.

JoJo takes her show on the road, performing in Blackpool, England, in 2018.

All the while, she was working on producing new music, and she dropped her *D.R.E.A.M. the Music* EP on Siwanatorz in 2018. The fizzy "D.R.E.A.M." is a standout—its aspirational lyrics and punchy choreography are both super-addictive. It's also a road map to achieving dreams laid out by someone who is living her dream every day. "We can do it if we see it / If you see it you can be it / You believe it you achieve it / You just D-R-E-A-M," JoJo suggests encouragingly. And the song's cheerleading-inspired dance moves reinforce the spirit of motivation.

By the Numbers

With her face in stores and all over the Nickelodeon network, JoJo's YouTube has become big business in its own right. *J-14* reported in 2019 that her YouTube channel earns **$9,600 a day** in ad revenues—that's a whopping **$3.5 million per year**!

In November 2018 JoJo announced via livestream that she would be embarking on the D.R.E.A.M. tour, and Siwanatorz everywhere rejoiced. The 27-city tour sold out completely just three minutes after tickets went on sale. By popular demand (obviously!), another 28 dates were added…and then 17 more…and then more and more, to bring the tour to 95 dates in North America, Europe, and Australia as of this writing.

The tour supports *D.R.E.A.M. the Music* as well as a new EP, *Celebrate*, and features tons of fun and surprises. At one point, JoJo zooms down a giant slide. At another, she disappears from the stage in a giant spray of confetti. There are several costume changes and set pieces that form an intricate narrative that incorporates multiple fantasy lands, a misbehaving puppy, a sparkly unicorn, and even a time-traveling bow. She worked with longtime Lady Gaga collaborator Richy Jackson, who choreographed new dance routines for the stage show. The super-intricate steps are perfect for JoJo, who's been dancing basically from the cradle.

JoJo also includes tributes to some of the greats. After seeing *Bohemian Rhapsody*, she became "obsessed" with Freddie Mercury. She was taken in by his incomparable showmanship and abundant talent. And she also saw a little of herself in him. "He was unapologetically himself…. He looked different than everyone. I've always been like that," she told *Time*.

As a nod to her newly minted hero, she incorporated some Mercury-esque touches into her own D.R.E.A.M. tour. She carries a special microphone mounted on a stick, just as the

JoJo's D.R.E.A.M. Playlist

Couldn't make it to the show? Try cuing up these tunes, which comprise JoJo's typical setlist during JoJo Siwa D.R.E.A.M. the Tour.

1. "Worldwide Party" by JoJo Siwa

2. "It's Time to Celebrate" by JoJo Siwa

3. "My Story" by JoJo Siwa

4. "Hold the Drama" by JoJo Siwa

5. "Every Girl's a Super Girl" by JoJo Siwa

6. "I Want Candy" by the Strangeloves (or check out the Bow Wow Wow version popularized in the 1980s)

7. "Tootsie Roll" by 69 Boyz

8. "Kid in a Candy Store" by JoJo Siwa

9. "Everyday Popstars" by JoJo Siwa

10. "Take Me Out to the Ball Game" by Edward Meeker

11. "High Top Shoes" by JoJo Siwa

12. "We Will Rock You" by Queen

13. "Another One Bites the Dust" by Queen

14. "We Are the Champions" by Queen

15. "Only Getting Better" by JoJo Siwa

16. "#1U" by JoJo Siwa

17. "Who Let the Dogs Out?" by the Baha Men

18. "A Friend Like BowBow" by JoJo Siwa

19. "Bop!" by JoJo Siwa

20. "D.R.E.A.M." by JoJo Siwa

21. "Boomerang" by JoJo Siwa

"When I find a piano, I play until my fingers won't let me play anymore."
—JoJo via Instagram

Queen front man did. (No surprise, she put her own stamp on it with the addition of rainbows and glitter.) She even performs a medley of Queen's greatest hits during the tour, including "We Will Rock You" and "Another One Bites the Dust," and bringing it home playing "We Are the Champions" at a glittering red, white, and blue piano (a nod to another great, Elton John, whom she had the privilege of meeting in 2019).

JoJo is known for her over-the-top style, enthusiasm, and performances, and the D.R.E.A.M. tour did not disappoint her Siwanatorz in these areas. Writing in a review of the performance for Jezebel.com, Julianne Escobedo Shepherd put it this way: "The kids in the audience roared and stomped their feet, juiced not just that their teen idol JoJo was finally there to regale them in all her sequined splendiferousness, but also because JoJo's holistic sparkling energy has the general overall effect of radiating out and making children lose their [minds]."

And if Siwanatorz have gone gaga for JoJo, it's for good reason. She may well be the hardest-working performer in Hollywood. ★

"I know I'm different from most 16yr olds, I know I dress different, I know I act different, I know people my age don't normally live life the way I live mine, but I get to do what I love 24/7 and I get to inspire the next generation of kids on such important incredible things like being kind, being confident, and having fun!"

—JoJo via Instagram

Living the D.R.E.A.M.

Siwanatorz around the U.S. and Canada had the opportunity to get up close and personal with their idol when JoJo announced the 2019 JoJo Siwa D.R.E.A.M. the Tour, which began in May 2019. Sponsored by Nickelodeon and Party City, the onstage extravaganza is stopping in 79 cities across North America and another 11 overseas. Were you lucky enough to nab a ticket?

Date	City	Date	City	Date	City
5/17/19	Phoenix, AZ	7/20/19	Mashantucket, CT	9/10/19	Memphis, TN
5/19/19	Los Angeles, CA	7/21/19	Queens, NY	9/11/19	New Orleans, LA
5/20/19	San Diego, CA	7/23/19	Boston, MA	9/13/19	Sugar Land, TX
5/21/19	San Jose, CA	7/24/19	Newark, NJ	9/14/19	San Antonio, TX
5/23/19	Seattle, WA	7/26/19	Uniondale, NY	9/15/19	Edinburg, TX
5/25/19	Eugene, OR	7/27/19	Philadelphia, PA	9/17/19	Grand Prairie, TX
5/28/19	Salt Lake City, UT	7/28/19	Lewiston, NY	9/18/19	Cedar Park, TX
5/30/19	Denver, CO	7/30/19	Pittsburgh, PA	9/20/19	Tulsa, OK
6/1/19	Tulsa, OK	7/31/19	Columbus, OH	9/21/19	Kansas City, MO
6/2/19	Kansas City, MO	8/2/19	Toronto, ON	9/22/19	St. Louis, MO
6/4/19	St. Louis, MO	8/3/19	Detroit, MI	9/24/19	Nashville, TN
6/5/19	Des Moines, IA	8/4/19	Milwaukee, WI	9/26/19	Duluth, GA
6/6/19	Minneapolis, MN	8/6/19	Omaha, NE	9/27/19	Greenville, SC
6/8/19	Chicago, IL	8/8/19	Broomfield, CO	9/29/19	Charlottesville, VA
6/9/19	Chicago, IL	8/10/19	Las Vegas, NV	10/1/19	Bridgeport, CT
6/11/19	Cleveland, OH	8/11/19	Santa Barbara, CA	10/2/19	Providence, RI
6/12/19	Baltimore, MD	8/13/19	Anaheim, CA	10/30/19	Glasgow, Scotland
6/13/19	New Brunswick, NJ	8/14/19	Oakland, CA	10/31/19	Manchester, United Kingdom
6/15/19	Hartford, CT	8/15/19	Reno, NV		
6/16/19	Lowell, MA	8/17/19	Portland, OR	11/2/19	Birmingham, United Kingdom
6/18/19	New York, NY	8/18/19	Redmond, WA		
6/20/19	Charlotte, NC	8/20/19	Vancouver, BC	11/3/19	London, United Kingdom
6/21/19	Nashville, TN	8/24/19	Lincoln, NE		
6/22/19	Atlanta, GA	8/25/19	Cedar Rapids, IA	11/4/19	Cardiff, Wales
6/25/19	Grand Prairie, TX	8/27/19	Grand Rapids, MI	11/6/19	Dublin, Ireland
6/26/19	Austin, TX	8/28/19	Kettering, OH	11/7/19	Dublin, Ireland
7/10/19	Orlando, FL	8/29/19	Rosemont, IL	1/11/20	Brisbane, Australia
7/12/19	Sunrise, FL	8/31/19	Wilkes-Barre, PA	1/13/20	Sydney, Australia
7/13/19	Saint Augustine, FL	9/1/19	Harrington, DE	1/14/20	Sydney, Australia
7/14/19	Charleston, SC	9/4/19	Toledo, OH	1/16/20	Melbourne, Australia
7/16/19	Greensboro, NC	9/6/19	Indianapolis, IN	1/17/20	Melbourne, Australia
7/18/19	Richmond, VA	9/7/19	Louisville, KY	1/17/20	Melbourne, Australia
7/19/19	Vienna, VA	9/8/19	Birmingham, AL	1/18/20	Melbourne, Australia

"Proud of my girl @itsjojosiwa...
You do the work, be a good
person, do right by those who
have your back & positive energy
in the world comes to you!
Inspiration for ALL."

—Richy Jackson
(@richysquirrel) via Instagram

chapter five

Express Yourself

Anyone who knows anything about JoJo can recognize her unique style. She's certainly not hard to miss when she walks into the room!

But just how did JoJo evolve her singular fashion sense?

It all began with the bows, JoJo's signature piece of flair going back to day one. "I've been wearing bows for my whole, entire life—since I was in preschool and obviously now and above and beyond," she told *Ad Age* in 2017. Jessalynn used to construct and bejewel them in their Omaha home, little pieces of bling to spice up her daughter's outfits and dance costumes alike. Before long, JoJo got in on the action herself, and the pair would spend quality time creating those looks together. These days, they still get after the BeDazzler, but they now have a huge room in their home devoted to crafting. Together, they create bows and outfits that end up on the red carpet and in music videos. They call it their rhinestone room, where they create JoJo's so-called "wow wear." Fans of JoJo's social media know it well, as she makes regular vlog appearances there.

Rocking a next-level
look at the 2019 Kids'
Choice Awards.

Showing off a head-to-toe flip-sequin ensemble at a 2018 concert in Sydney, Australia.

So what about the clothes? A huge influence on JoJo's aesthetic has to be her unbridled love for the fashion of the 1980s. "I love the 1980s," she wrote in *JoJo's Guide to the Sweet Life.* "My theory is that I was actually born in the eighties and the government transplanted me to present day. Just check out the way I dress if you need proof." The iconography and patterns that she gravitates toward are pure '80s cheese too, such as the appliques she wears on her bomber jackets, checkerboard patterns, neon colors, and hearts and stars and unicorns...just to name a few. So too is her signature choice of footwear—the high-top shoe—which became a serious fashion statement for women in the 1980s.

Take Madonna's oversized hair bows, Cyndi Lauper's tutus and rainbow-splashed hair, and Cher's insatiable love of all things sparkly, and that gives you an idea of JoJo's sensibility. "The JoJo aesthetic is Midwestern Bob Mackie:

rainbow sequin separates, machine-washable tulle, hearts and stars and unicorns," reports *Time*. (Mackie, incidentally, was the designer who created many of Cher's iconic, mega-sequined looks in the 1980s.)

But it's not just the ladies of the '80s; JoJo takes cues from some of the all-time musical greats. On her D.R.E.A.M. tour, she rocks a fully sequined baseball uniform, a clear homage to Elton John and his famous star-spangled L.A. Dodgers outfit. Her feathered look from *The Angry Birds Movie 2* premiere is another nod to Sir Elton. The hot-pink jumpsuit she wears in the music video for "Bop" is a purposeful tribute to idol and Queen singer Freddie Mercury. (She's also rocked a bedazzled version of the yellow jacket Mercury wore in Queen's historic 1986 Wembley Stadium show.) Onstage, she wears glittering face paint reminiscent of David Bowie during the Ziggy Stardust era. Lady Gaga is one of JoJo's favorite contemporary fashion influences, a glittering star who takes major fashion risks and isn't afraid to stand out. (It was Gaga who said that

> "What do people want me to do, wear black every day?"
>
> —JoJo to *Time*

Wearing the Elton John–inspired look to throw out the first pitch at a 2019 Chicago Cubs game.

Crimped hair? Check. Studded denim vest? Check. Blue eye makeup? Check. Rainbow neons? Check. Touching all the '80s bases at her 13th birthday party.

she wants to change the world one sequin at a time; little wonder that JoJo wants to follow in the diva's footsteps.)

And while all of these influences play into JoJo's aesthetic, she has a vision that is singularly hers. Who else can pull off an elaborately sequined gown, a high ponytail, and athletic shoes with the same ease as a unicorn onesie? Fashion is at root a form of self-expression, and JoJo's style is simply inimitable.

Fans who love JoJo's outfits can get the look in stores such as Target, but JoJo reminds them that it's always best to stay true to their own sensibilities. When asked by *Justine* magazine if she has advice for Siwanatorz in putting together an outfit, she said bluntly: "Just be yourself. My style is my style, your style is your style." ★

Did You Know?

August 19 is International Bow Day. What better way is there to celebrate than rocking a JoJo bow?

Sequins: A Timeline

14th Century BCE: When King Tutankhamun's tomb was discovered in the 20th century, so too was the earliest known sequin. The pharaoh's mummified body was wrapped in various garments that had flat gold disks sewn to them. The gold ensured that Tut would be wealthy in the afterlife, in accordance with ancient Egyptian beliefs.

7th Century BCE: The earliest known coins in Islamic society are minted. The silver coins, called *sikka*, are thought to be the origin of the word *sequin*.

13th Century: Venetian mints begin producing *zecchino*, gold coins, which were often sewn inside travelers' garments. *Zecchino* is another possible origin of the word *sequin*.

1480: Leonardo da Vinci draws plans for a sequin-making machine. Like many of his visionary ideas, this one was never realized.

17th Century: The sequin becomes used in decoration on clothing as an ostentatious display of wealth. Besides being a lavish expense in and of itself, the construction of a sequined garment is incredibly labor-intensive.

1930s: Sequins used to decorate clothing and other apparel are made from gelatin. Resources are plentiful, as animal bones are often discarded in meat production. However, the sequins are not of high quality; they melt in high heat and dissolve in water (and thus can't be washed). On the plus side, they are edible!

1940s: Sequin pioneer and luxury atelier Herbert Lieberman of Algy Trimmings Inc. revolutionizes sequin production when he realizes he can make them from acetate. Working with Eastman Kodak, he uses the same material that the company uses for its film stock.

1952: DuPont invents mylar, which is used to coat the acetate sequin and add a little extra sparkle.

Late 20ᵗʰ Century: Ultimately, vinyl becomes the most widely used material for sequins. It's cheaper, more durable, and easier to mass-produce.

2016: The flip sequin craze hits the children's apparel market.

2018: JoJo's Closet premieres at Target. The first capsule collection includes replicas of some of JoJo's most recognizable outfits—all featuring sequins and other embellishments.

"There is no other person. I literally am JoJo. I wear the bright clothes every day. I wear the sparkly hair bows. I wear the high-top shoes. I sing the fun music. I talk really loud. I talk fast, and I talk a lot. This is who I am."

—JoJo to *Time* on her on-screen vs. off-screen persona

chapter six

She Works Hard for the Money

No discussion about JoJo Siwa would be complete without addressing her massive merchandising empire. She has literally turned her ethos of being herself into a global brand.

The immensity of her accomplishment is not lost on her. "There has never really been someone who has done what I've done," she told *Time* in 2019. "I'm live-action. I'm the first real-life license—the first human, who is not playing a character, to be licensed as a brand."

The centerpiece of that brand is, of course, the bows. The meaning behind them makes them more than just a fashion statement. And they're far from a passing fad. Consider this: they even landed JoJo on the front page of the *New York Times* Style section, ordinarily reserved for high-fashion ateliers. More than 7,000 different styles of bows have been produced to date, and they come in every conceivable color and pattern. They're available everywhere from Claire's to Target to Dollar General. Put simply, the demand has been overwhelming (she sold 40

Many of JoJo's fans come to concerts and appearances wearing JoJo products.

JoJo speaks during Nickelodeon's presentation at Licensing Expo 2018.

million of them in 2018 alone!).

What started with the bows has ballooned into something else entirely, and it's big business. Recent estimates for the 16-year-old's net worth

By the Numbers

Siwanatorz unite! JoJo reported in May 2019 that she had sold a whopping **60 million** bows worldwide.

range from $10 to $12 million, but with a world tour in full swing as of this writing, and more and more products rolling off the assembly line, those numbers are climbing ever higher.

More is more for JoJo, whether it's putting together an outfit or putting out new products for her fans to enjoy. And unlike some celebrities, who leave the decision-making to others, she is involved in every aspect of her merchandising. That's equally true when it came to creating her logo. "You might not know this, but my logo is a combination of a Heart, Infinity sign, and a Star," she explained via Instagram in 2019. "They each represent something special... The Heart represents loving everyone, The Star represents being different (no 2 stars are the same), and the Infinity Sign represents being you forever!"

Dream Crazy Big!
The JoJo Siwa Story

JoJo's social media presence seamlessly functions as a platform to introduce Siwanatorz to new products. In addition to regular tours of the merch room at the Siwas' residence, which holds every imaginable JoJo-related product on the market, JoJo often makes vlogs of herself and Jessalynn cruising the aisles at Target, Party City, and other retail stores, browsing the shelf for her wares.

First, there's the clothing. Target's JoJo's Closet line features reproductions of some of JoJo's most memorable outfits, including red-carpet and music-video looks. JC Penney has a line of JoJo Siwa apparel, including graphic tees, leggings, and even leotards. Kohl's carries her swag, as does Walmart, Justice, Carter's, Macy's, and Nordstrom Rack, among others. You can even buy a JoJo Siwa Box

JoJo celebrates her 14th birthday by giving away free merch at a Walmart in Rogers, Arkansas.

Sporting her logo apparel in Las Vegas.

directly from Nickelodeon. Each surprise box, available as a onetime purchase or as a subscription, contains exclusive apparel and merchandise.

But that's just the tip of the iceberg. There's also food, bedding, party supplies, plush dolls, action figures, underwear, kitchenware, games, scooters, watches, jewelry, cosmetics, shoes, hats, sunglasses, bags, craft and bow-making kits,

Mega Mentor

Having Kim Kardashian West, the master of self-branding, on speed dial isn't something most teenagers can boast, but then JoJo's no ordinary teenager. They initially connected through West's oldest daughter, North, an enthusiastic Siwanator. "Kim is one of the sweetest people I have ever met.... She's given me some very good words of advice," JoJo told *Today* in 2019.

Dream Crazy Big!
The JoJo Siwa Story

school supplies, hair extensions, mobile games, and even (as you might expect from a Nickelodeon personality) slime! She even released an exclusive 24-piece capsule collection with Amazon for Prime Day. And there are books ranging from coloring and activity books to her best-selling memoir. The list goes on and on.

JoJo has made big business out of having fun. And why shouldn't she? Her products are a reflection of her. She wears the clothes, she sports the bow—it's a part of who she is IRL (that's "in real life," to the uninitiated). Put simply, "she lives, breathes, and literally drinks her brand," as *Rolling Stone* writes.

Siwanatorz everywhere have responded to that authenticity, and their desire for all things JoJo only seems to be growing. ★

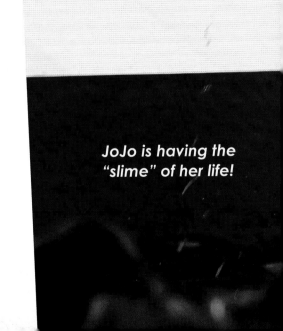

JoJo is having the "slime" of her life!

Rainbow Connection

JoJo has hundreds of bows in her personal collection, and has worn one in every shade of the rainbow. Here are just a handful of her greatest hits!

Crushing it in orange in 2016.

In Vikings purple at the 2018 Super Bowl Experience in Minneapolis.

Pretty in pink at the 2015 Kids' Choice Awards.

Bringing a little sunshine to the 2017 Macy's Thanksgiving Day Parade.

Sporting a white bow and rainbow extensions at her 13th birthday party.

Aqua blue on a 2018 red carpet.

JoJo's version of black tie.

"Slime" green at the 2017 Kids' Choice Awards.

Why wear one color when you can have the whole rainbow?

Rocking red on WE Day in 2017.

"It does not matter if I have a billion dollars or if I have two dollars. If I'm happy and if I love what I'm doing, that's what matters."

—JoJo to *Today*

Sweet Dreams
(Are Made of This)

These days, there seems to be no stopping JoJo. She's a top-flight social media influencer—she was even named one of *Time*'s Most Influential People on the Internet in 2019.

She's killing it onstage, with a sold-out tour reaching three continents. She's a regular personality on Nickelodeon, a familiar live-action *and* animated face. She's a *New York Times* best-selling author. She even made her first foray into feature films when she voiced not one but two characters in *The Angry Birds Movie 2*. Perhaps most impressive, she's a brilliant marketer; you can hardly go anywhere without seeing her merchandise.

Is there anything the teenager *can't* do? Margaret Kramer, writing in the *New York Times*, doesn't think so. "JoJo's millions of followers on various social media platforms, consumer-product empire and sold-out concerts are reason enough

In full-feathered regalia at The Angry Birds Movie 2 premiere.

The sky's the limit for the young superstar.

Chapter Seven
Sweet Dreams (Are Made of This)

to believe she is just getting started," she reported.

Maybe the secret to JoJo's success is that she is loving every minute of it. "I'm doing what I love, with the people that I love, for the people that I love! It's the perfect life.... I couldn't ask for anything better!!" she wrote on Instagram in 2019.

Some observers worry she'll soon outgrow her childlike persona, but JoJo doesn't concern herself with that too much. Like everything else, she has a plan for that. When asked by Music Choice in 2018 what her five-year plan was, she had a ready answer. Not content to rest on her laurels, she wants to be a musical

Dream Crazy Big!
The JoJo Siwa Story

artist on world tour, become
an actor in a family-friendly TV
show, and become a humongous
YouTuber. After just a year,
she's already accomplished two
of those goals, along with many
more achievements. Could a
regular TV gig be far behind?
Considering she has an overall
talent deal with Nickelodeon, the
stars seem aligned.

Wherever the road takes her,
her fans understand what
defines JoJo first and foremost:
she stays true to her authentic
self. And if history has been
any indication, Siwanatorz will
follow in the footsteps of her
high-top shoes. ★

"My absolute dream come true [would be] going to stadiums, having 70,000 people at a show. That would be incredible."
—JoJo to Fox News

Onstage during JoJo Siwa
D.R.E.A.M. the Tour.

Search Party

There are so many ways to describe JoJo. She's nothing if not one of a kind! Search the grid below to find the terms in the word bank. Words may appear forward or backward and horizontally, vertically, or diagonally.

A	P	M	B	O	R	E	M	A	E	R	D
L	E	N	G	W	K	F	A	O	C	K	N
U	R	O	L	E	M	O	D	E	L	R	I
G	F	I	X	J	Y	R	B	M	E	R	O
O	O	R	C	D	O	A	E	B	V	Q	D
M	R	A	E	T	R	N	U	H	O	A	T
R	M	M	A	C	E	T	L	R	N	E	G
J	E	E	H	E	U	Y	N	C	W	X	H
N	R	E	V	O	L	T	E	P	E	C	O
C	J	R	Y	W	S	R	E	G	N	I	S
R	E	C	N	E	U	L	F	N	I	O	T
B	H	I	N	N	O	V	A	T	O	R	E

WORD BANK

CREATOR
DANCER
DREAMER

HOST
INFLUENCER
INNOVATOR

MOGUL
PERFORMER
PET LOVER

ROLE MODEL
SINGER
YOUTUBER

"I'm 16 and I'm living my life exactly the way I want to. I think having my dream career at age 16 is really cool. No matter what anyone says, you can tell me I dress young, you can call me bald, you can say I'm annoying—nothing will change me!"

—JoJo via Twitter